HAL•LEONARD®

VIOLIN

PLAY-ALONG

AUDIO
ACCESS
INCLUDED

VOL. 1

BLUEGRASS

To access audio visit:
www.halleonard.com/mylibrary

Enter Code
7752-5043-6505-0366

Recorded at BeatHouse Music, Milwaukee, WI
Fiddle by Jerry Loughney
Guitars by Bill Brenckle
Double Bass by Brian Baker
Banjo by Jon Peik

ISBN: 978-1-4234-1377-6

Visit Hal Leonard Online at www.halleonard.com

HAL•LEONARD®
CORPORATION
7777 W. BLUEMOUND RD. P.O. BOX 13819
MILWAUKEE, WISCONSIN 53213

VOL. 1

HAL•LEONARD®
VIOLIN
PLAY-ALONG
AUDIO ACCESS INCLUDED

BLUEGRASS

CONTENTS

Foggy Mountain Breakdown

By Earl Scruggs

(Banjo solo)

mp

(end Banjo solo)

(Banjo solo)

Gold Rush

Words and Music by Bill Monroe

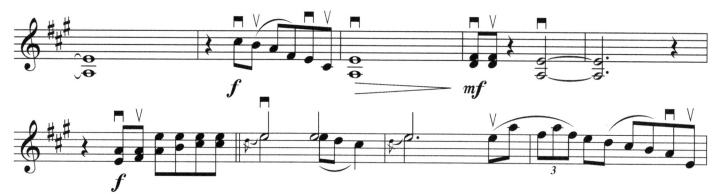

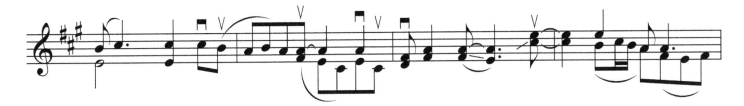

simile

D.S. al Coda

Coda

John Hardy Was a Desperate Little Man

Words and Music by A.P. Carter

Moderately bright

(Guitar solo)

Orange Blossom Special

Words and Music by Ervin T. Rouse

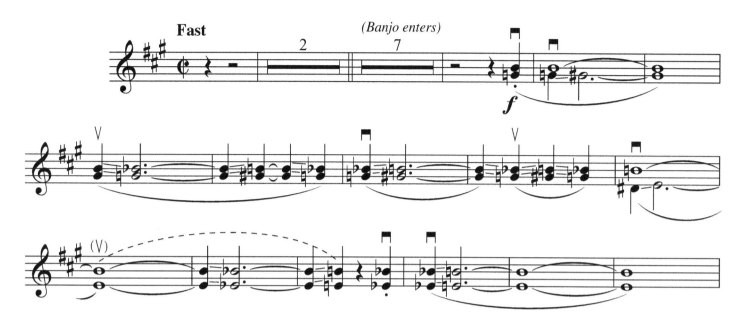

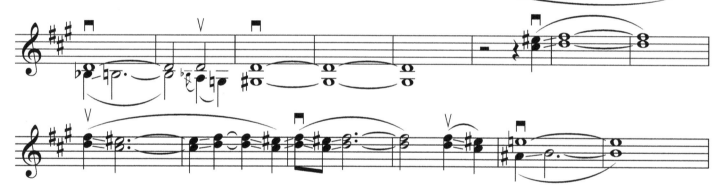

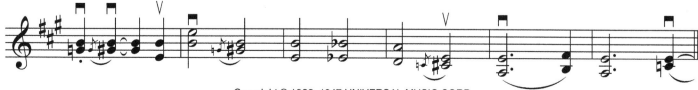

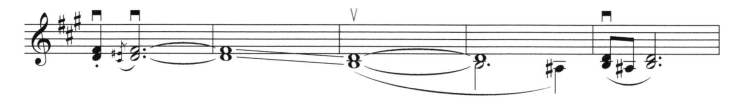

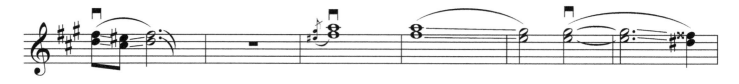

Salty Dog Blues

Words and Music by Wiley A. Morris and Zeke Morris

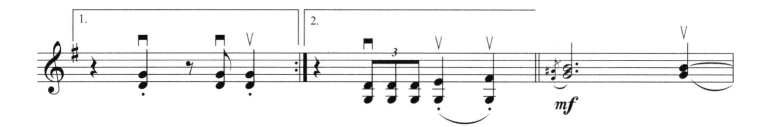

Tennessee Waltz

Words and Music by Redd Stewart and Pee Wee King

You Don't Know My Mind

Words and Music by Jimmie Skinner

Moderately bright

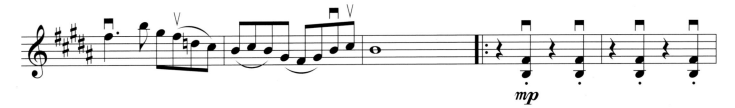

Panhandle Rag

Words and Music by Leon McAuliffe

Moderate Country Swing

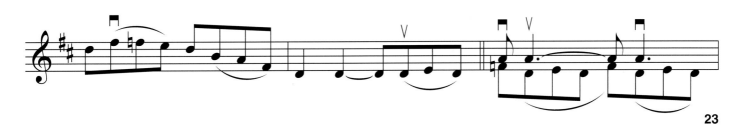

D.S. al Coda

Coda